Pandemic

Pandemic

By David Kherdian

CASCADE PRESS

Text Copyright © 2020 by David Kherdian
Cover illustration by Lusine Ghukasyan

All rights reserved.
No part of this book may be used or reproduced in any manner whatsoever without written permission, except in the case of brief quotations embodied in critical articles and reviews.

Published by Cascade Press
under exclusive license from David Kherdian.

Kherdian, David. Pandemic.
Summary: Poet David Kherdian shares his thoughts on the pandemic of 2020 through simple, unobtrusive verses, providing grace, prayer, and deliverance for those in need.

ISBN paperback 978-1-64872-008-6
ISBN hardcover 978-1-64872-009-3

Inquiries regarding permissions or bulk printing requests should be sent to info@cascade.press

For the latest updates and news about publications, be sure to sign up for our newsletter at www.cascade.press

To our recovery and continuance
with a new appreciation of one another,
this planet, and all its beings,
to live and grow and evolve

Contents

HERE NOW	9
CLOUD	10
CLYDE	11
OUR PANDEMIC	12
QUESTION	14
MOUNTAIN AND MEADOW	15
NEIGHBORS MAYBE	16
APRIL 6, 2020	17
TIME NOW	18
THE ANSWER	19
TO WRITE A POEM	20
WHAT THEN	21
US	22
APRIL GREEN	23
ORCHIDS 2	24
BUZZ	25
ARK	26
EASTER	27
EASTER EVE	28
DOGWOOD	29
HELLO	30
DISCOMBOBULATED	31
THE WIDOW ACROSS THE STREET	32
FOR NONNY'S 88TH BIRTHDAY	34
STILLNESS	35
BLESSINGS	36
AND THEN	38
CONSCIENCE	39
NOW AND TOMORROW	40
AWAKENING	41
THE MOMENT	43
AND NOW	44
NOW	46

HERE NOW

Now the days hunker down
and the luminous moment appears
there beyond my window:
two very small dogs slowly being walked—
a wonder, to see how large
little things are now,
with all of life seemingly hung on a string—
memory vanishing when there is only now

The mind wondering in amazement,
the heart in hurt, buried in feelings unsorted
it cannot own or understand,
and now we see, for the first time,
that nothing can exist apart

That everything that breathes could
breathe its last at any next moment,
to alter this next breath of mine—
for we are not two breathes alone
and apart, but one breath held by two,
to make one life, that cannot be separate
but must join, if life is to endure,
one day to find and grow our God.

CLOUD

When a cloud billows
up gigantically before us,
seemingly from the earth,
like a great gray being,
looking down on us—
as sometimes happens,
unexpectedly

reducing us to size,
for being of a substance
we cannot hold or explain,
that belongs to another god,
to remind us that there
are forces and powers
all about us that cannot
be fathomed or blown away

or disregarded—
these spheres that do
or do not include us,
that simply appear and disappear—
as we will one day,
in an hour not so different than
this mysterious moment now,
not to be explained
as we cannot.

CLYDE

The neighbor's dog
pathetically alone, walks,
head down across the next
door lawn, feeling lost,
concerned by the quiet
that surrounds—
something has grown
odd and no one and
nothing knows why—
he is mute with the
question, and the world
cannot tell him why.

OUR PANDEMIC

This is what happens
when tragedy strikes, as
surely this pandemic is—

certain private rituals
begin to occur, and time slows
for us to understand:

a walk twice around
the inner rooms of our home
in the evening hour

drinks again at an exact
hour, and meals un-missed
routinely taken, no longer

with the flavor of surprise;
exactly performed,
and each day the hours tighten

and time slows to a crawl.
We hug each other more often
and claim our love

and gratitude for what has
already been, and think about
what may come to be—

for we are no longer busy with life,
and very un-busy with ourselves.
Tomorrow we may lean on the porch rail,

and maybe wave up at the sky
that is always there, wondering
how long we might have to go

so let us make due, offer love
wherever we can,
our time might be at hand,

and if not remember
this hour
for the time ahead.

QUESTION

Still, life goes on,
cheerfully as before,
the three small bushes
fronting out house
are coming into bloom—
our first spring here,
so new to us.

We watch their green leaves
sprout, witnessing again
the miracle of spring,
knowing that what is continues,
anew, renewed,
to flow and flower again,
for us to trust that we
are not done,
that a virus can only
slow us down,
not eliminate us
as it seems bent on doing—

What is the lesson to carry
away from all of this:
ask and answer and question
but do not give up.

MOUNTAIN AND MEADOW

All else failing, no one to visit—
every door closed, with everyone in hiding,
we took a long drive through the countryside.
and to our amazement we came
to a beautiful meadow,
under view of the standing mountain here—

But something was missing—lost time,
leaving us to imagine this meadow
as something other than a silent green
empty expanse of land only—wanting
instead to see a teepee again, and Indians:
naked, free, alive and at home,
here among the natural things that have
endured their passing—

But with little to show for it:
some unhappy cars here and there, cows,
and one lone pony being scrubbed and
washed by two shirtless youngsters,
standing in for all that was once here.

NEIGHBORS MAYBE

The youngish woman across
the road from us sits in silence
on her porch, almost hourly now,
when even in cold weather she
comes to sit for hours alone,
having recently married
only to lose her husband, who died
suddenly, just after they moved
from the house we are now in,
to the one we are facing across from us.

And this is all we know of her,
as she is private and aloof,
choosing to shun us,
and so we have never met her or her dog,
who, like her is equally silent, and
never barks, and is nearly always
curled obediently at her side.

And there they sit,
a young widow on her porch,
in a home with a dog, and little more;
assured apparently, of a way of life
the pandemic may never seriously
disturb—alone in quiet
across from our living room window,
were by daylight she is ever in view,
though cannot see us.
What strange creatures we are,
in this time that grows stranger
by the hour.

APRIL 6, 2020

Ah, the colors,
soft and pink and
quiet green,
that now hesitatingly
appear in trees
and bushes, their
voices subdued
barely noticed
but with presences felt.

This is life appearing in
its time—
without notice,
or in need of praise—
here, suddenly
near, a beauty,
welcomed dearly,
not knowing the words
to say how,
only the wordless feelings.
of enveloping love.

TIME NOW

In the midst of all this
the shadow of death
comes to sit over us,
making even the most
ordinary of things
stand out for noticing,
life now a filter into the unknown,
and even the commonplace
takes on an eerie quality,
defying itself, everything now
suddenly unreal.

THE ANSWER

Why is it death alone can
solve the mystery of life
when to go there is to
leave both mystery and life;
ponder the imponderable
do not pick its leaves,
or the tree will come down
with a different dread, an
unrecognizable sound.

TO WRITE A POEM

What we don't know
is how much we know,
wherever it lies,
needn't come as surprise

your arm ready for
the unknown known
to flow down its arteries
pencil poised to write it all down

as it flows from rivers
unnamed,
inside this body
whose mystery yearns to be plumbed

let it be, let it see,
whee! watch and wait and
wonder, don't be alarmed

you are the Colossus
without a name, or need
to be claimed for renown

your pencil ready, the
world in place
to crown over all that trusts
and believes and waits.

WHAT THEN

What is this dull quiet
that ensues, to embrace us
while the outer slowly disappears

a new ether is entering now
and we are between
life and death

suddenly understanding neither—
both appearing
before us as a mirage

a stage set, for us to give
it life with our life,
that we imagine we always had—

the stage seen now, again,
where once we were alive
but did not Exist.

US

People continue to walk along
this road-like street of our home,
some with dogs,
presumably to frighten the bears
who do not care—
we don't even annoy them,
they are above all that,
but now these and other worries
are taking command in this
insidious silence we are captured in
that is covering the land—
our invisible enemy everywhere,
and nowhere to be found—
leaving us to fall back on ourselves,
and to face the enemy we have run from
all our lives—ourselves, our bloody selves.

APRIL GREEN

The green sprouts that came
magically, out of their
broken stubs of branches—
having stood there naked all
winter long outside our window—

Are now spreading their wings
as it seems—
to say, if they could in words—
what words, however can never describe—

So seek thou ever outside
of time and language
for what all life yearns for
which is more life.

And that is its meaning—to live,
toward its final meaning, which is beyond us,
however much we yearn
as poet, observer, seer or securer of love—
for what we know is not all we know—

Say yes and turn your check
away, for yet another day.

ORCHIDS 2

Are the orchids weary,
perhaps impatient
with our longing for them
to stay—as they are—
as we are

they in their corner,
we across the room,
watching, entranced,
for what is ours on loan—

random particles of time
alone with them,
seeking wholeness and
beauty and life and light.

BUZZ

We've been buzzing and
buzzing and buzzing
and now at once we have
been stopped,
and not by our intelligence
but another's
to breathe in another day
as if it was the first,
and it is, for there are
many firsts, so how
many have we reached
and how can we tell the
last first from the one before
if we cannot tell the dancer
from the dance

So try to find the conductor
in the wings,
arranging the rhythms
only the planet knows,
for us to catch the flow,
unheeding unknowing
unwilling participants in a drama
not for us to understand
but to live in pain and agony
and finally with remorse
that reconciles, only
from an understanding hard earned
by each and everyone of us,
arriving where we are headed.

ARK

Where is the ark
that will carry
us over from this—
with kindness and mercy,
that have always been
in short supply,
everyone for oneself,
dog eat dog the mantra
we grew up with eighty
and still more years ago,
with nothing changed since;
not that history repeats
itself, but that mankind
cannot change—unless faced
with such a catastrophe—
out of desperation—feeling
another's misery through
their own, rising to meet
the call; but how high,
on whose legs when
our own stumps have been
without compassion or
aid for others throughout
all of their lives—
Covid-9 perhaps a final chance,
so don't miss it, there may not be
another, for you to save yourself.

EASTER

Will we crack eggs
for Easter,
which is not to be
delayed,
and if not celebrated—
if that is the right word—
will we remember

will we not forget
earlier times of rituals
and ceremonies and
other interruptions we
didn't care for as children but
could not escape.

And all of it again—now
in memory, for it is hard to
remember what could be lost,
when survival is uncertain
and the days ahead a blur

And finally, what do we
have to look forward to
if the best of what
was past is past, when what
lies ahead is uncertain and for
now in dread.

EASTER EVE

What do I believe has been learned
from all of that which has happened,
yanking us out of our usual passivity
and chaos, from which it had appeared
there would never be an escape

But instead from out of all this,
I believe again that goodness matters,
and that through its realization we
will find that all is one.
It has begun to take place in
the hospitals, but can spread far
beyond, if we seize this moment
with open hearts and minds,
and find impersonal love—

What it means to love our neighbor as ourself,
this goodness, which comes from
a spiritual home inside our beings,
has risen before in emergencies such as this,
to correct our worst features of self love,
competitive greed and blindness to the needs
and rights of others

Becoming a million islands rising up
out of a wild, incoherent and turbulent sea
to become a single continent heeding a call
that must be heard by all.

DOGWOOD

Our dogwood is blooming,
the flower ahead of
the leaf, that follows
gallantly behind, proud
of its place—
for look at what is
being glorified on earth,
of which its leaf is an
indispensable part,
this most beautiful
of trees

and here we have one
in our own front yard
we renters—
are we all not renters—
in our little hatches,
hoping for renewal
too, this spring,

our own life to
flower anew
yearning and hoping for
its continuance,
beseeching helplessly for another
day followed by the next,
just continuance, wanting suddenly,
nothing more than this.

HELLO

To this bush-like shroud,
outside our window,
bare and brown and ignored
all winter,
its naked branches
suddenly adorned with new leaves,
transforming it in every way

Like a new beauty
arrived in the neighborhood
that everyone wants to meet
and know, and to have her hello.

Ah world, we are here,
as inscrutable as the tiniest worm,
that, too, has its place
in the over-all.
Breathe in breathe out
this is yours, ours,
for we are also from God.

DISCOMBOBULATED

Now we know what it may mean,
this happening, this unresolvable
occurrence that must be lived,
not solved,
for we are not its willing partner
or even a portion of this thing
that we cannot understand,
but instead
we are its unprepared, and seemingly
unwarranted victims
of something we are choiceless
to receive, that is perhaps
not unlike our deepest problems,
that own us until understood, suffered
and given an earned release,
by our own forces,
from this force seemingly outside of us,
when in fact there is nothing outside of us,
but only this misunderstood, unearned
and therefore unowned side of us
that one day we must conquer
once we understand and are understood.

THE WIDOW ACROSS THE STREET

The dog sits on its haunches
and watches her,
she who never reads,
sitting silently on her porch,
day upon day,
talking to no one unless
in her head, there just
across the street from us,

But being loners ourselves—
my wife and I—
we understand, are in agreement
with her, for whatever reasons
she may have or not have
that are in common with us.

It is a lonely world,
this world we live in now,
with vague hopes things will warm
up somehow—
even if no direction is to
be found—which is what
she tells me with silence,
irrevocably better than
what the talkers are saying now.

Be silent then, do not utter a word,
and try to remember love,
once clearer than any remark;
with those too pained to speak,
wanting a return to something
they may once have dreamt of.

FOR NONNY'S 88TH BIRTHDAY

MAY 7, 2020

A vase sits on the end table,
flowers pink, white and yellow,
Nonny's birthday present
arriving from afar;
everything distant now,
including what is near
here in our shutdown site

Not a candle or cake to put it on,
for me to light, and Nonny to cheer,
such it is, but the indomitable beauty
of life will not be stilled

The clarion call from the distant
hills sounds even louder now,
for being blessed in quiet,
the heart surrendering at last,
for eternal love to appear
from out of the dark

Free in this day where nothing
is clear but the love we hold
that will not give way to what
threatens its life,
that no death will ever put asunder.

STILLNESS

There is a stillness now
that is new,
apart from the usual
nervous agitation
over what comes next
and what to do,
as if life was waiting
for us, when it is we
who must take on life, although
uncertain of the future,
having lost our assurance,
our presumption
that life is always there.

Now to be grateful for life,
and concerned over
the welfare and safety
of others,
a new beginning,
something never practiced,
unfamiliar, yet not radical
in thought, but sudden,
surprisingly necessary, for even
when isolated we are not alone,
but connected to others
who are now just us,
as we now are forever theirs.

BLESSINGS

Blessings we always see as gifts
from out of the blue,
often coming to us in surprise,
and never as a thing we might
not know anything about,
for that is how we are made
looking always on the bright side,
because we do not want to suffer,
only feel delight,
deserving the best, worry-free,
a carefree life,
without question or strife

So what are we do with this present gift
that we can neither swallow nor justify,
or find any excuse for inside ourselves,
but that we must live through if able—
this unasked for guest
who doesn't need us to make room for itself,
shaking us to our core,
and with no intention of leaving
a calling card, either as invitation
or instruction,
or as a gesture in parting,
choosing to leave in its time

Because Nature doesn't do that
nor its parent God,
nor even their many angels—

for here, on our island, although
descended from beyond,
realizing that we must sweat and suffer
intentionally, whether we understand
our selves or not—
to endure this test, not as mere
playthings of God,
but as visiting agents who need
testing, and praying and serving to work
our way to the glory we have as yet
no understanding of.

AND THEN

Now I remember,
we used to play catch,
like the boy
across the street with
his mother.
How was it then—
a ball, two gloves
the ball sailing
in the air, interrupted
by a gloved catch
some chatter,
not anything anything but this,
with a silent shroud,
always above
our heads in the air,
that we could feel silently,
watching us and
the ball, that once traveled
from boy to boy—
how long are we going to be here?

CONSCIENCE

It is the moment when
you see that this life is
not about you, but that you
can become something for it
in a way of service;
a challenge to be grasped or lost,
perhaps forever.

We are tested every day
and do not see this—
but there are moments,
periods, occurrences
that put us to the test,
revealing this certainty,
alerting our conscience to go
forward into what we are seeing

Or we will be lost on our journey—
and nothing that happens after this
can release us from the bonds
of conscience, that is our
connection to the Higher,
that is ever in us, that if kept to
will one day bring us to God.

NOW AND TOMORROW

What is this sense of loss we feel but
the losing of the familiar—
the life we think we have that is ours;
a false assurance, when we see
that we take the outer shell of life
as something we own,
and that this something is us—

When it is really a false construction
of life that we will shed at death,
to see truly who we are,
and the life we lost in living,
if that living was not real because
we were not real,
but a mockery, now to accept
and live with—

But the part of us that is true
can see this now, and not be shattered,
once the shell we were held in together
begins to crumble
and our false sense of security is
seen as such, and our suffering
shouldered—facing the eternal,
to realize that the gift we were given
can be taken away at any time.

AWAKENING

The day my name was given to me
by an Indian shaman, was, in a sense the
first day of my life, for it made plain
and understandable my pattern,
my potential, to accept and follow my destiny.

Such moments rarely come our way in the
course of our time, and unless we have been
in a spiritual school, the likelihood
that life itself will reveal and deliver us
to this place—and with such seeming magic—
seems very unlikely at best.

But thinking back, and then forward to where
we are now, I see, if only faintly,
that we can all break through to the other side,
as was once said long ago in a 60's lyric,
because now the shutters that have closed
over our eyes, to keep us, like trained sheep
to our pens, in a pattern and program, to
cover over us irremediably.

But this planet in its slow evolution requires all this,
but now come moments of wakefulness, when our sleep,
and our hibernation from reality—with its complete
obedience to this mechanicality that has hypnotized us
and rules our sleep—can now, from out of this present crisis,
reveal to us how weak and defenseless we are, but from

Out of this struggle we can awaken to this luminous moment,
to understand what it means for us,
and what our possibilities are, always inherent,
to awaken us, to become truly human,
but not for the first time, but Hu man (God man)—
as once we were and can become again.

THE MOMENT

There is that moment
in the day when
the earth exhales
its last breath,
for the arrival of the next

lifting us out of ourselves,
yearning, perplexed,
suspended in time—
between what is here
and what lies beyond.

AND NOW

It is a quiet that has no name,
or gesture, to declare itself with,
so our searching minds and troubled hearts
want to find messages in the twirling leaves
that shield the sun from us, as it absently
falls over and above this rotating globe,
its seeming fall without volition
or seeming purpose to our eyes,
and as bound and gagged as we are,
just doing its little—very big—thing.

And does it believe as we do
that all is well in our glorious world,
that we sometimes delight in, or kick against
in our confused and continuing passage,
of which we understand so little
while having no seeming control over its rise and descent,
or anything else.

Is its consciousness so great that we cannot enter
into it in partnership, and share its truth?

And now, more than ever before, right now,
we are losing our bearings,
because everything is new again,
and we are not children, nor wise, nor knowing
what might come next, having imagined
or believed, hesitatingly, that we were

in partnership with God and all that is real,
whether with our understanding or another's;
to believe in, and with faith and hope—
the lifeline that is now slipping through our hands.

NOW

Now we become Human
or else—
this is not a warning
but a correction,
on a model unseen,
but ours nonetheless

To learn what it takes,
how hard it is
to pass from one level
to the next

Facing blindly the enormity
of this planet, the Sun our god,
this earth our playground
if we are to become
its qualified emperor

To lead what is here to the light,
knowing as yet so little of its life,
while slowly earning the right
to understand it better,
to live here consciously,
and play the part we are lost in now.

ABOUT THE AUTHOR

David Kherdian is the author and editor of over seventy books, that include poetry, novels, memoirs, biographies, retellings, and children's books. His anthologies include *Beat Voices*, and three seminal works: *Down at the Santa Fe Depot: 20 Fresno Poets*, that inspired a series of regional anthologies, *Settling America: The Ethnic Expression of 14 Contemporary Poets*, and *Forgotten Bread: Armenian American Writers of the First Generation*. With his wife, two-time Caldecott Medalist, Nonny Hogrogian, they were the publishers of three small presses, and as editor / art director, three disparate journals: *Ararat: A Quarterly*, *Forkroads: A Journal of Ethnic-American Literature*, and *Stopinder: A Gurdjieff Journal for Our Time*. He has, with his presses, journal and anthologies, along with his own work, helped place ethnic writing into the canon of American literature.

His many awards include the Newbery Honor Book, The Friends of American Writers Award, the Boston Globe / Horn Book Award, the Jane Addams Award, a nomination for the American Book Award, and two lifetime achievement awards: The Emily Lee Award, and The Armenian Star Award. His translations and retellings include the Asian Classic: *Monkey: A Journey to the West*. An hour-long documentary of his poetry and life by filmmaker Jim Belleau was released in 1997, and can now be seen among his Youtube appearances.

www.ingramcontent.com/pod-product-compliance
Lightning Source LLC
Chambersburg PA
CBHW021125080526
44587CB00010B/642